Milet

Picture
Dictionary
English·Japanese

Text by **Sedat Turhan**

Illustrations by **Sally Hagin**

COLOURS/COLORS
色

red
赤

orange
だいだい色

yellow
黄

green
緑

blue
青

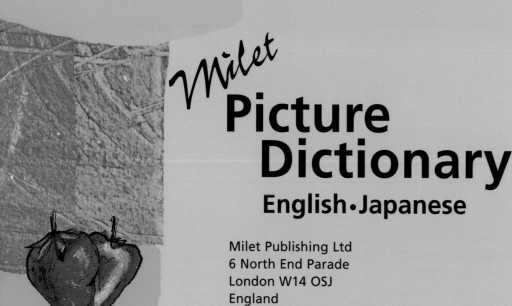

Milet
Picture
Dictionary
English·Japanese

Milet Publishing Ltd
6 North End Parade
London W14 OSJ
England
Email info@milet.com
Website www.milet.com

First published by Milet Publishing Ltd in 2003

Text © Sedat Turhan 2003
Illustrations © Sally Hagin 2003
© Milet Publishing Ltd 2003

ISBN 1840593555

Printed in Belgium

purple
紫

grey
灰色

pink
桃色

black
黒

white
白

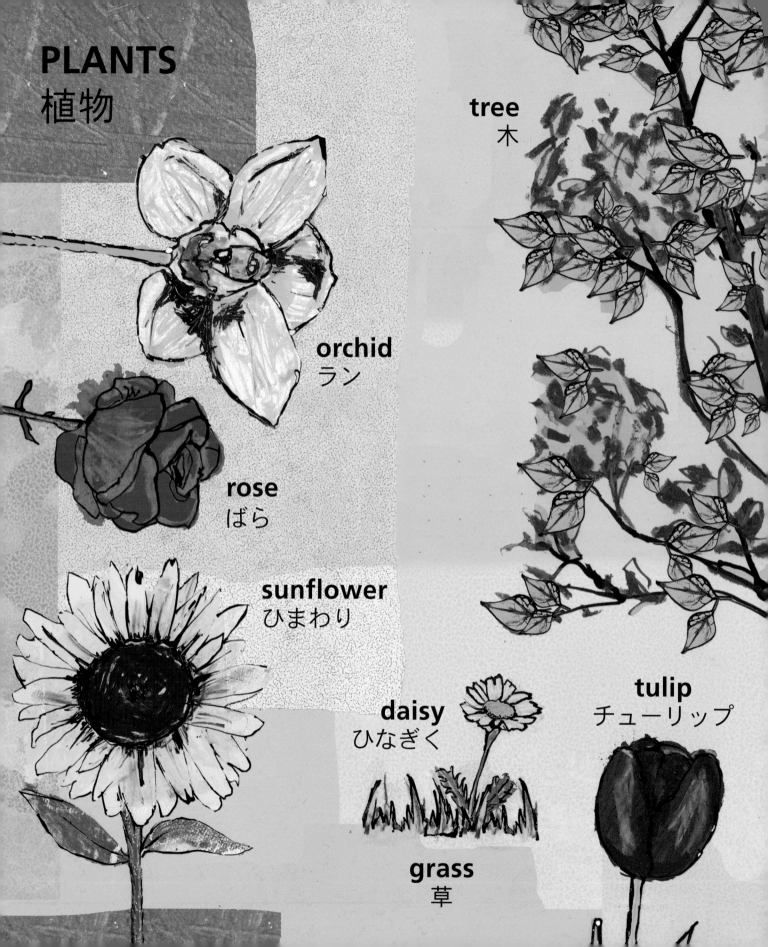

PLANTS
植物

tree
木

orchid
ラン

rose
ばら

sunflower
ひまわり

daisy
ひなぎく

tulip
チューリップ

grass
草

lily
ゆり

branch
枝

leaf
葉

daffodil
すいせん

watering can
じょうろ

cactus
サボテン

plant pot
植木鉢

FRUIT
果物

kiwi
キーウィ

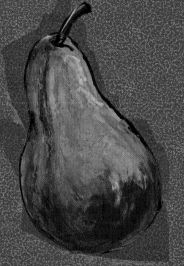

cherry
さくらんぼ

apricot
あんず

pear
なし

fig
イチジク

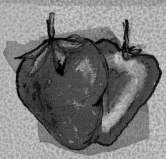

strawberry
いちご

peach
もも

banana
バナナ

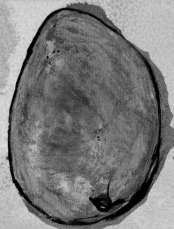

mango
マンゴ

orange
オレンジ

apple
りんご

blueberry
ブルーベリー

lemon
レモン

grapes
ぶどう

avocado
アボカド

raspberry
キイチゴ

grapefruit
グレープフルーツ

pineapple
パイナップル

ANIMALS
動物

lion
ライオン

zebra
しまうま

tiger
とら

giraffe
きりん

elephant
ぞう

penguin
ペンギン

duck
あひる

polar bear
北極ぐま

cow
牛

rooster
おんどり

goat
やぎ

sheep
ひつじ

horse
うま

ANIMALS & INSECTS
動物と虫

bird
鳥

dog
いぬ

cat
ねこ

rabbit
うさぎ

frog
かえる

crab
かに

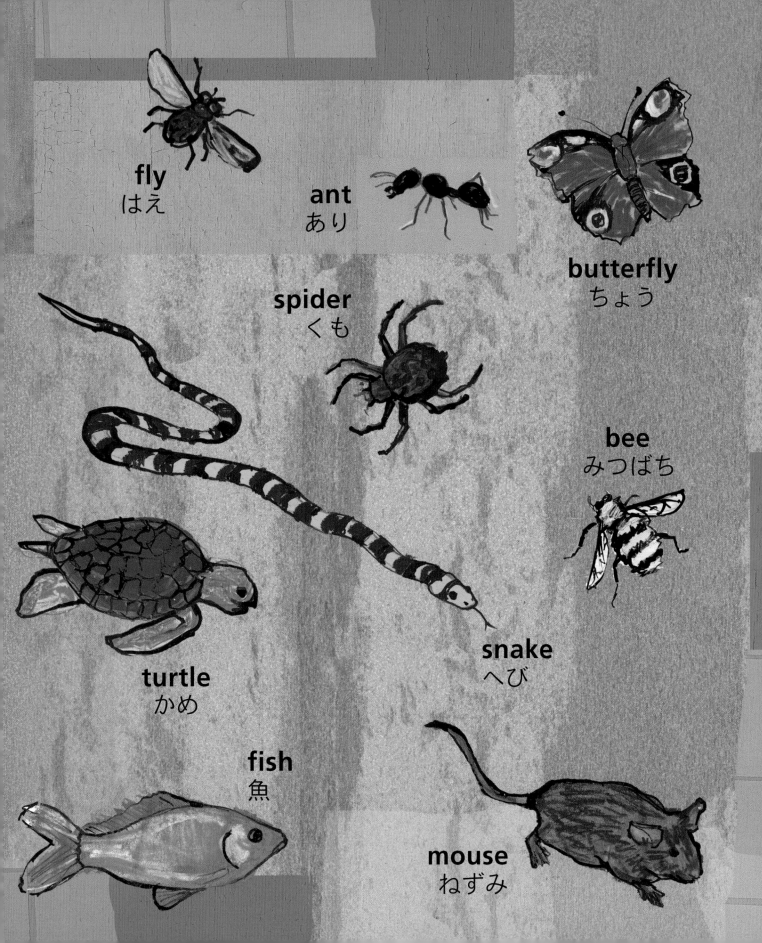

fly
はえ

ant
あり

butterfly
ちょう

spider
くも

bee
みつばち

turtle
かめ

snake
へび

fish
魚

mouse
ねずみ

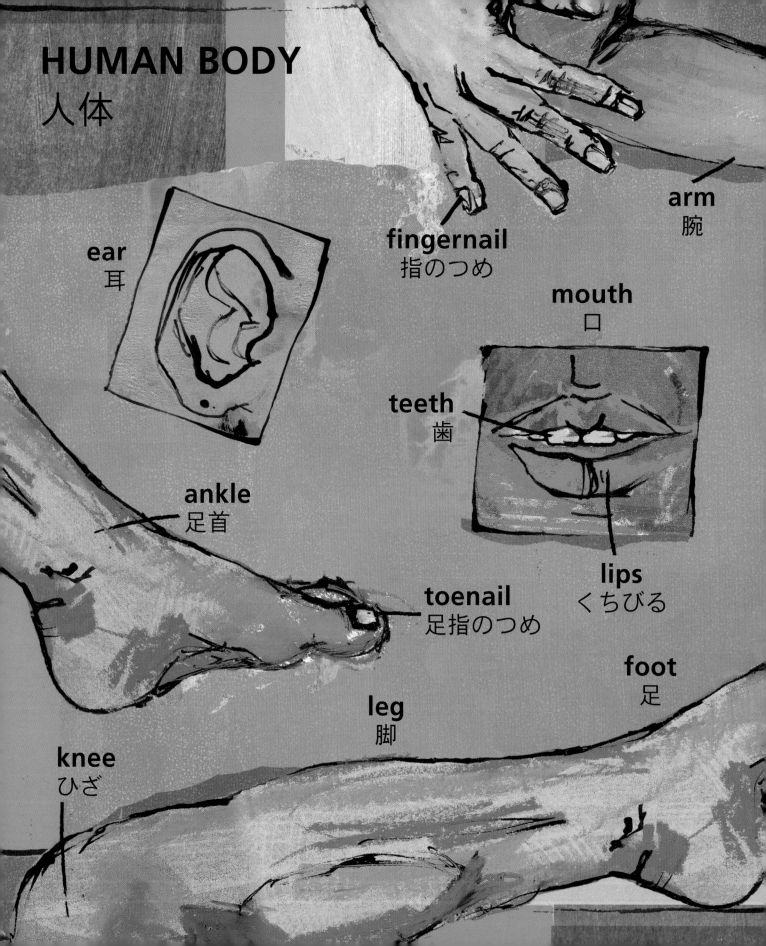

HUMAN BODY
人体

arm
腕

fingernail
指のつめ

mouth
口

ear
耳

teeth
歯

ankle
足首

lips
くちびる

toenail
足指のつめ

foot
足

leg
脚

knee
ひざ

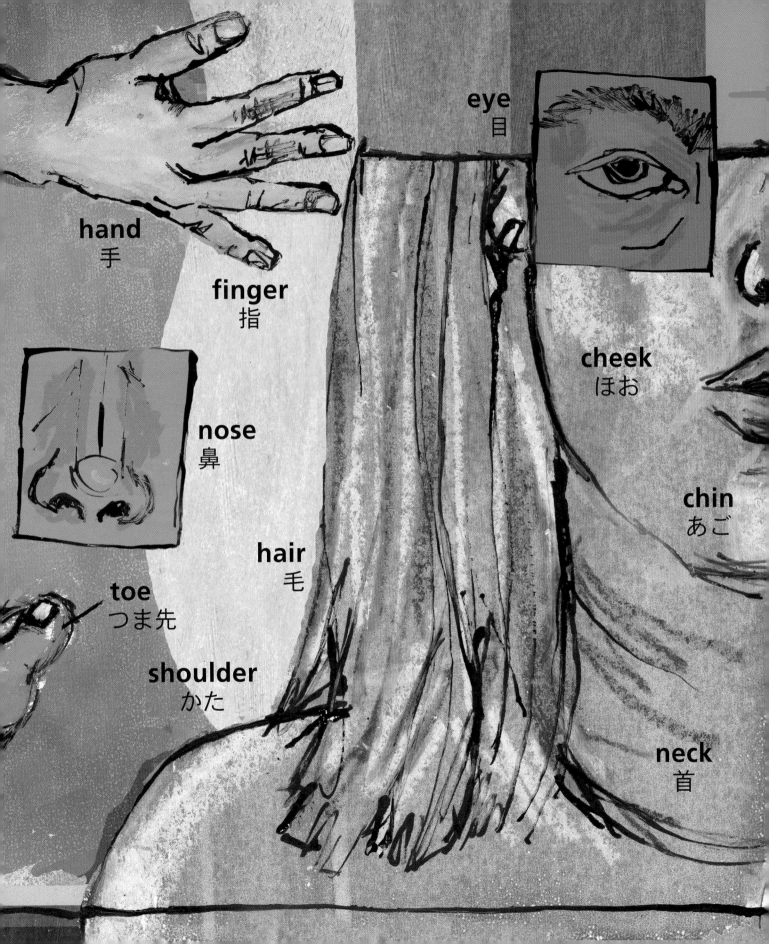

hand
手

finger
指

nose
鼻

toe
つま先

shoulder
かた

hair
毛

eye
目

cheek
ほお

chin
あご

neck
首

HOUSE & LIVING ROOM
家と居間

house
家

chimney
えんとつ

roof
屋根

door
戸

key
かぎ

candle
ろうそく

light bulb
電球

armchair
ひじ掛けいす

picture
絵

bookshelf
本だな

cabinet
キャビネット

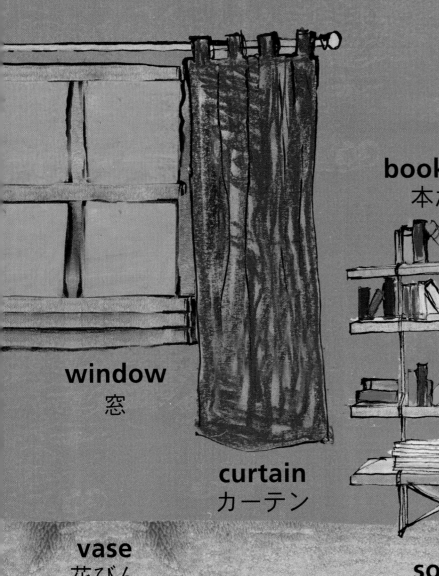

window
窓

curtain
カーテン

vase
花びん

sofa
ソファー

lamp
電気スタンド

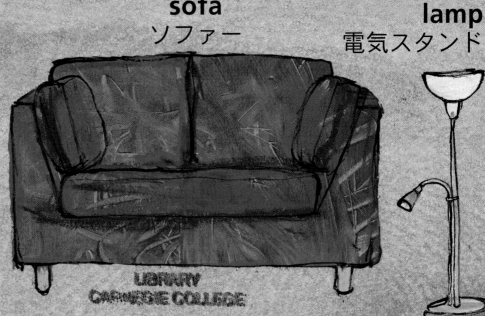

side table
サイドテーブル

LIBRARY
CARNEGIE COLLEGE

KITCHEN
台所

bowl
深皿

glass
コップ

refrigerator
冷蔵庫

plate
皿

napkin
ナプキン

teapot
急須

cup
カップ

table
テーブル

chair
いす

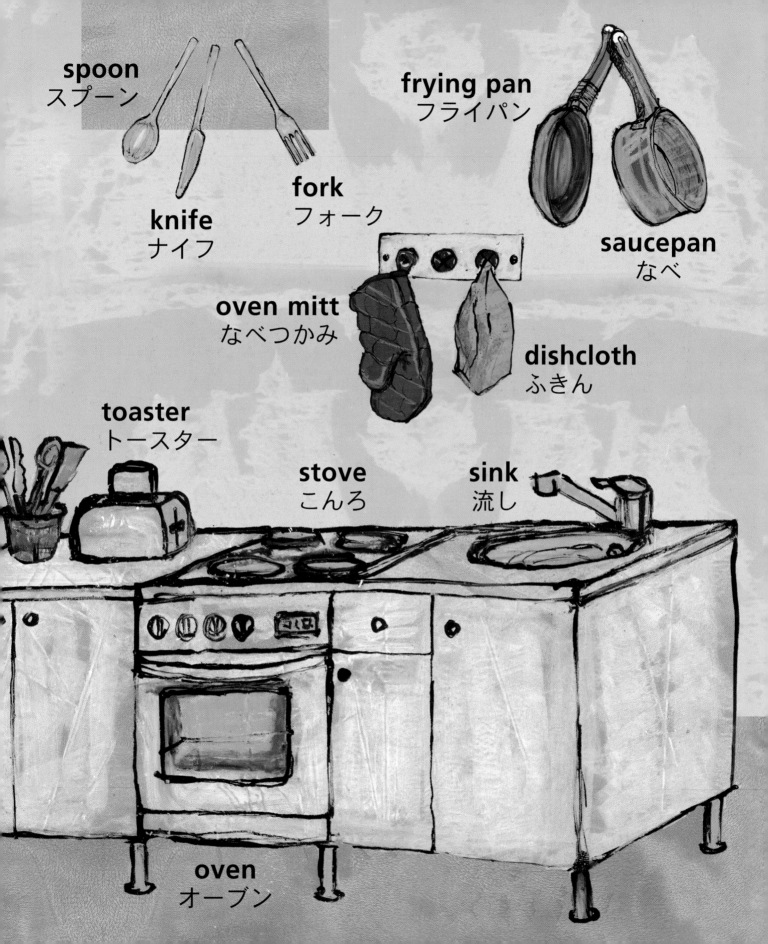

VEGETABLES
野菜

potato
じゃがいも

green bean
さやいんげん

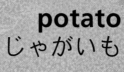

mushroom
きのこ

asparagus
アスパラガス

carrot
にんじん

onion
たまねぎ

pumpkin
かぼちゃ

peas
グリーンピース

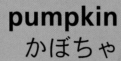

broccoli
ブロッコリー

okra
オクラ

tomato
トマト

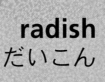

radish
だいこん

garlic
にんにく

cucumber
きゅうり

corn
とうも
ろこし

pepper
ピーマン

cauliflower
カリフラワー

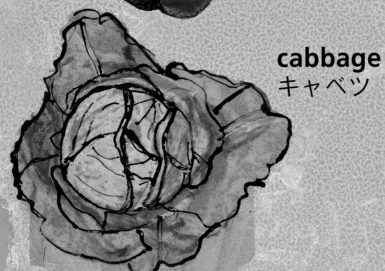

cabbage
キャベツ

FOOD
食べ物

 **sandwich**
サンドイッチ

 **bread**
パン

cheese
チーズ

 **milk**
牛乳

 **butter**
バター

 **jam**
ジャム

honey
はちみつ

 **egg**
卵

cereal
シリアル

raisins
レーズン

oil
油

fries
ポテトフライ

spaghetti
スパゲッティ

fruit juice
フルーツ
ジュース

chocolate
チョコレート

cake
ケーキ

ice cream
アイスクリーム

BATHROOM
浴室

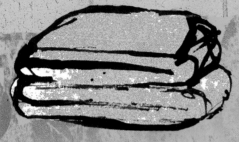

towel
タオル

mirror
かがみ

sink
洗面台

toilet paper
トイレットペーパー

toilet
トイレット

bathroom cabinet
浴室の戸だな

potty
おまる

hairbrush
ヘアブラシ

hairdryer
ヘアドライヤー

shower
シャワー

comb
くし

toothpaste
練り歯みがき

shampoo
シャンプー

conditioner
コンディ
ショナー

toothbrush
歯ブラシ

soap
石鹸

bathtub
浴そう

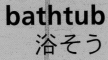

BEDROOM
寝室

bed
ベッド

alarm clock
めざまし時計

bedside table
サイドテーブル

hanger
えもん掛け、
ハンガー

rug
敷物

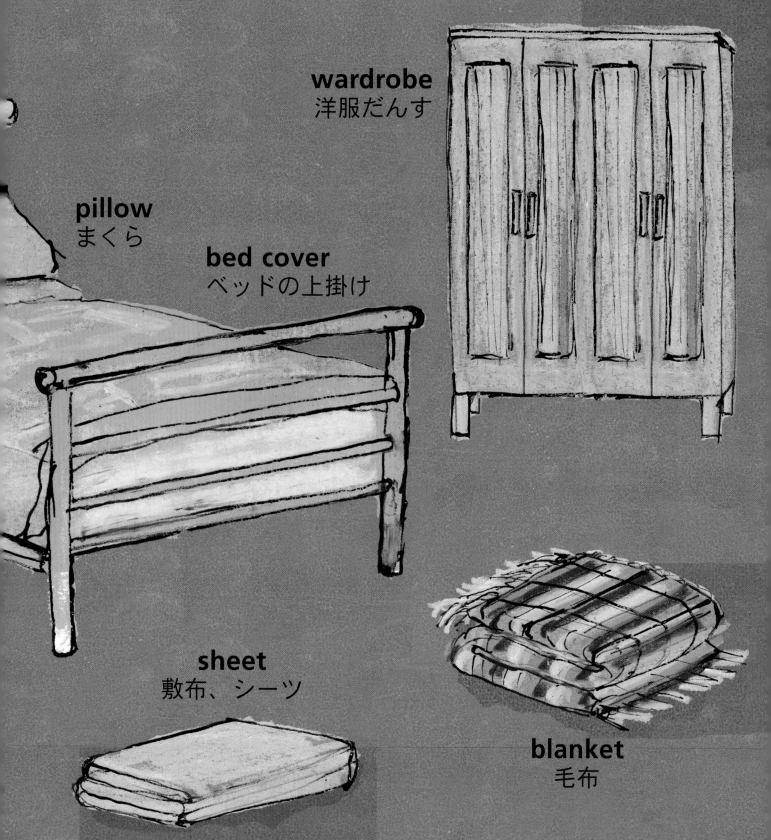

wardrobe
洋服だんす

pillow
まくら

bed cover
ベッドの上掛け

sheet
敷布、シーツ

blanket
毛布

CLOTHING
衣服

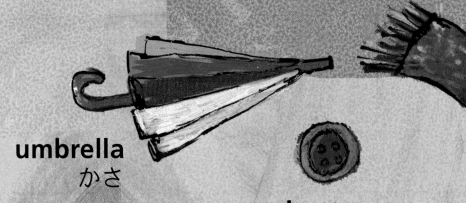

umbrella
かさ

gloves
手袋

button
ボタン

glasses
めがね

boxer shorts
ボクサーショーツ

T-shirt
ティー
シャツ

underpants
パンツ

hat
ぼうし

jacket
ジャケット、
上着

sweater
セーター

slippers
スリッパ

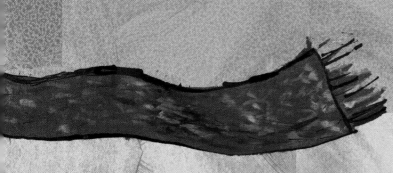

scarf
えりまき

backpack
リュックサック

skirt
スカート

shirt
ワイシャツ

handbag
ハンドバッグ

socks
ソックス、
短い靴下

belt
ベルト、バンド

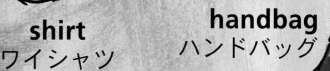

jeans
ジーン、ジーパン

pyjamas
パジャマ

shoes
くつ

shorts
ショートパンツ、
半ズボン

COMMUNICATIONS
通信

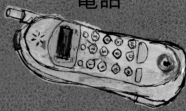

telephone
電話

television
テレビ

DVD player
DVDプレーヤー

video recorder
ビデオプレーヤー

remote control
リモコン、
リモートコントロール

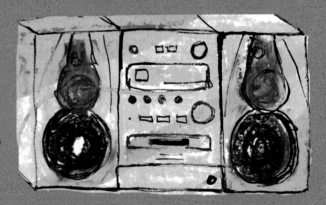

stereo
ステレオ

video camera
ビデオカメラ

camera
カメラ

TOOLS
道具

screwdriver
ねじまわし、ドライバー

screw
ねじ

saw
のこぎり

stepladder
段はしご、
きゃたつ

nail
くぎ

drill
電気ドリル

hammer
金づち、
ハンマー

shovel
シャベル

vacuum cleaner
電気掃除機

paint
ペンキとはけ

SCHOOL & OFFICE
学校とオフィス

pencil
鉛筆

glue stick
棒状のり

book
本

marker
マジックペン

stamp
切手

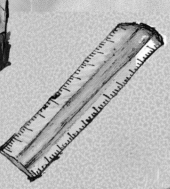

ruler
定規

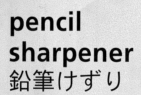

pencil sharpener
鉛筆けずり

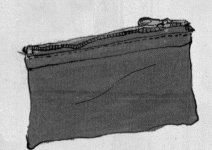

pencil case
ふでばこ

crayon
クレヨン

globe
地球儀

scissors
はさみ

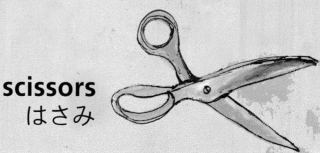

calculator
計算器

stapler
ホッチキス

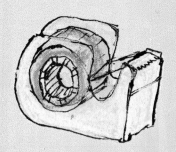

tape
テープ

paints
絵の具

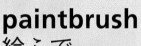

paintbrush
絵ふで

pen
ペン

envelope
封筒

computer
コンピュ
ーター

desk
机

notebook
帳面、ノート

NUMBERS
数

one
いち

two
に

three
さん

four
し

five
ご

six
ろく

seven
しち

eight
はち

nine
く

ten
じゅう

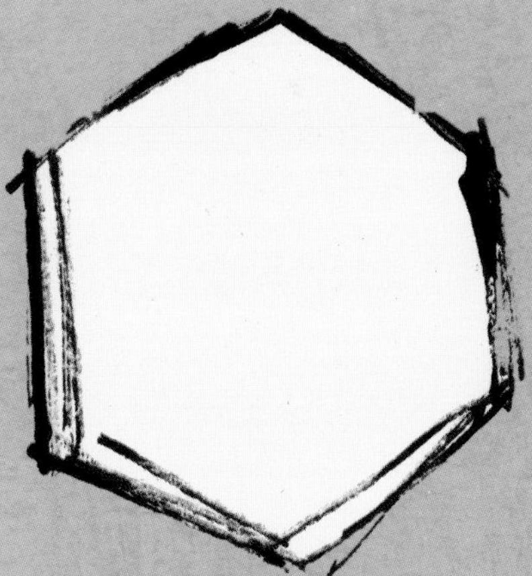

hexagon
六角形

rectangle
長方形

square
正方形

oval
楕円形

circle
円

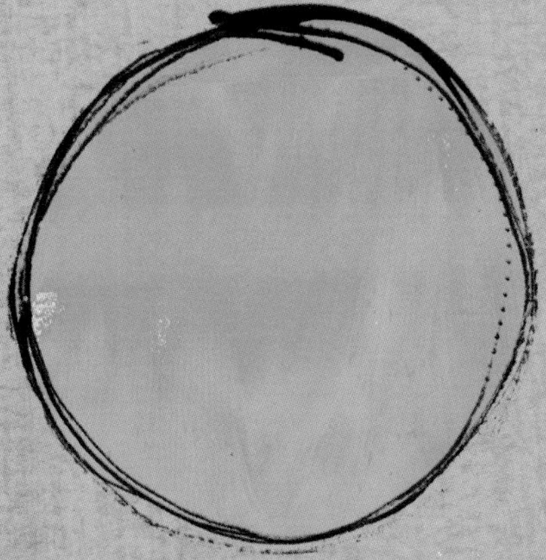

triangle
三角形

octagon
八角形

MUSICAL INSTRUMENTS
楽器

flute
フルート

guitar
ギター

violin
バイオリン

saxophone
サクソホーン

bongos
ボンゴ

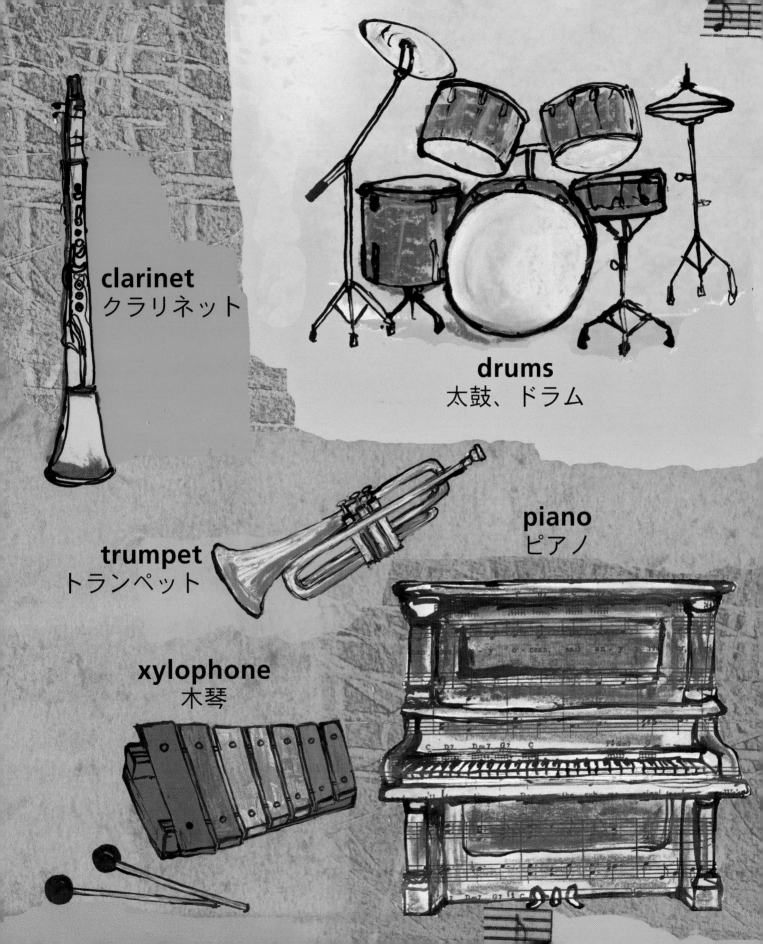

clarinet
クラリネット

drums
太鼓、ドラム

trumpet
トランペット

piano
ピアノ

xylophone
木琴

SPORTS & GAMES
スポーツと競技

skateboard
スケートボード

video games
ビデオゲーム

cards
トランプ

**football /
soccer ball**
サッカー
ボール

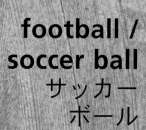

ice skates
アイススケート靴

rollerblades
ローラーブレード

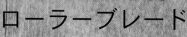

skis
スキー板

chess
チェス

baseball
野球

glove
グローブ

basketball
バスケットボール

bat
バット

American football
アメリカンフットボール

tennis ball
テニスボール

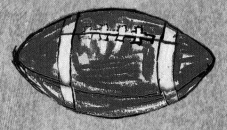

cricket ball
クリケットボール

tennis racket
テニスラケット

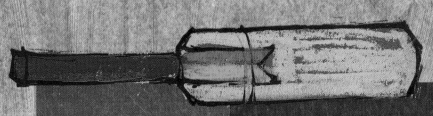

cricket bat
クリケットのバット

TRANSPORTATION
乗り物

boat
ボート

bicycle
自転車

train
電車

car
自動車

motorcycle
オートバイ

ambulance
救急車

helicopter
ヘリコプター

plane
飛行機

fire engine
消防車

bus
バス

truck
トラック

tractor
トラクター

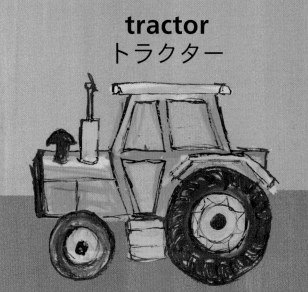

SEASIDE
海辺

ball
ボール

sky
空

beach towel
ビーチタオル

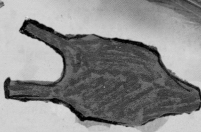

swimsuit
水着

beach bag
ビーチバッグ

sunglasses
サングラス

sunscreen
日焼け止めクリーム

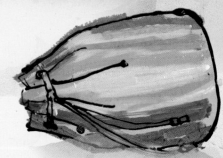

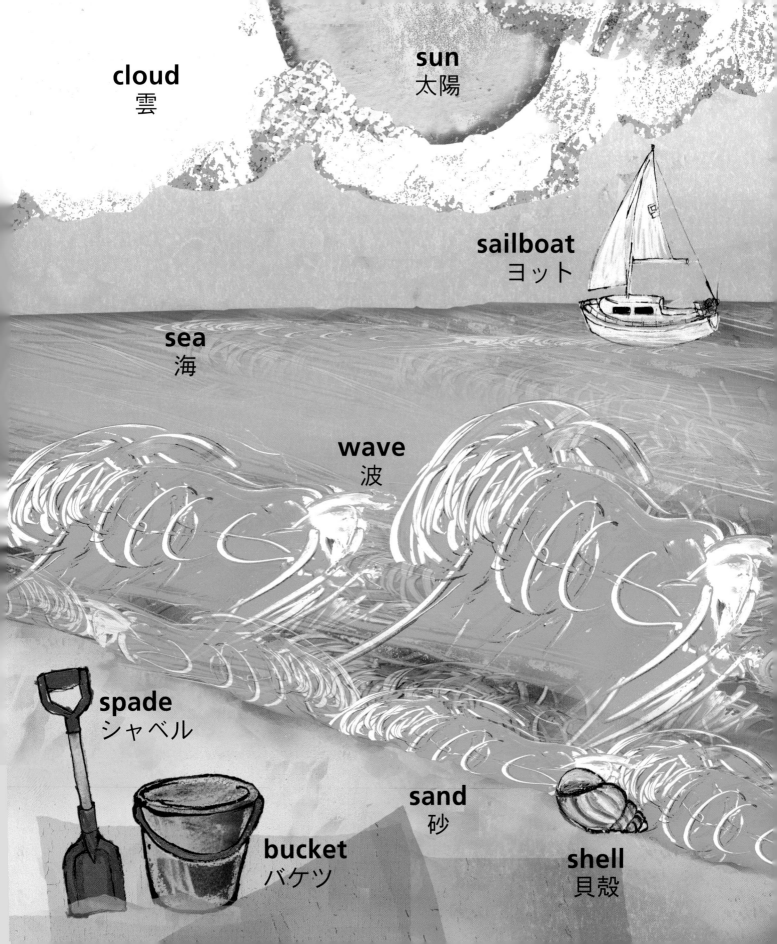

cloud
雲

sun
太陽

sailboat
ヨット

sea
海

wave
波

spade
シャベル

bucket
バケツ

sand
砂

shell
貝殻